Israel Poems

Rabbi Menachem Creditor

Israel Poems

2024 Edition, *First Printing*
© 2024 Menachem Creditor
Foreword © 2024 Alden Solovy
Cover photo © 2024 Raya Creditor

All rights reserved. No part of this book may be reproduced or transmitted in any form or by means electronic or mechanical, including photocopying, recording, or by any information storage and retrieval system, without permission in writing from the author.

ISBN: PP/ 9798325200137

for Am Yisrael

"Those who don't know how to weep with their whole heart don't know how to laugh either."

Golda Meir
Prime Minister of Israel (1969-1974)

"Happiness is to want what you have. Hope is to want something else. We have to see the good because that gives us the strength to keep going. We have to see the bad because that gives us the strength to change."

Tehila Friedman
Member of Knesset (2020-2021)

"We owe it to our past to not lose hope. Say what you will, despair is not the solution. Not for us."

Elie Wiesel
"Against Despair" (1979)

Israel Poems

CONTENTS

9	Foreword by Alden Solovy
11	Introduction

Book One: Before

17	jerusalem syndrome (in tel aviv)
19	the streets of tel aviv
21	crosswalk minyan
23	Gnarled Roots in Tel Aviv
25	here alone
27	why do i tremble?
29	a moment of radical normalcy
31	hoping between sobs
33	two minutes
35	this bench
37	one year later
39	committed to home: 5 years, 2 years, and 1 year ago today - and today
45	68 Words, 68 Years
47	still there
49	defiant rugelach
51	ice cream prophets
53	A Prayer After a Terror Attack in a Jerusalem Synagogue on International Holocaust Remembrance Day
55	tears and hope
57	j. l. gordon st: a one-street poem

59	Jerusalem at 6am
61	aromatics: the jerusalem syndrome
65	Our Cherished Litany of Loss
69	mall poems
73	the prophets' boutique
75	missing my own heartbeat
77	Kotel Poem

Book Two: October 7

81	A Prayer from a Traumatized Jewish Heart
83	What I See
85	Fractals of the Broken
87	Upon Bearing Testimony to Atrocities Committed Against Am Yisrael
89	Upon My Heart
91	Nova Poem #1
93	The State of our Heart
95	this is not the end
97	So That They Will See
99	Nova Poem #2
101	October Rain ("Hurricane")

foreword

Alden Solovy

Israel is poetry and song. When the poet or the musician enters into the land, verses rise within us. Israel has inspired thousands throughout the generations to pick up pen and pad. From King David to Yehudah Amichai, from Zelda to Rivka Miriam, Israel demands the writing of the poetic heart. That power cannot be bound. Israel also inspires from afar. Resonances from this ancient land of beauty and sorrow – this place from which God and holiness issue forth into the world – stirs artistic hearts everywhere.

The horror of October 7 – that still unbelievable Shabbat Simchat Torah – brought a painful energy into the heart of Israel poetry. From the moment I emerged from the bomb shelter in my Jerusalem apartment building, after the first air raid siren of the day, my artistic energy was bound into the terror and the tears. I was compelled to write: compelled by the land, by the tragedy, for our people. It is not a surprise that the artistic heart of Rabbi Menachem Creditor was catapulted and energized into bringing poetry into the world. Menachem spearheaded the publication of several collaborative volumes of poetic responsa in support of Israel. *This volume is different.* This is a book directly from his heart, and his heart alone.

My budding friendship with Menachem solidified on a hot summer morning in Israel. Of course, in Israel. It was Rosh Chodesh, the beginning of the new month of Av. We stood and prayed in support of Women of the Wall, holding firm against verbal abuse – and thrown objects – from opponents of prayer equality at Judaism's holiest site. When I asked Menachem to write the foreword to my first book from CCAR Press, his response was gracious and his words beautiful. Sharing that cover with him was an honor. Sharing this volume's cover with him, is an honor doubled.

Israel Poems is a personal journey in poetry. It's intimate and warm. We walk with Menachem through the streets of our land. He makes the mundane holy. He coaxes us to see with fresh eyes. Then, in the second section of the book, Menachem takes us into the pain of October 7, raw and unvarnished, wounded yet powerful. *Israel Poems* should be read as an invitation into the heart and soul – the prayers and dreams – of a profoundly sensitive man.

As a people, we have always found comfort, perhaps even answers, in words. Poetry will continue to rise out of the love, the pain, the fear, and the hope, we feel for this place. Israel demands it. Israel continues to inspire. No doubt that Menachem, and each of us, will continue to write. May we reach a day when all of us who write for, about, and because of Israel – Israel the land, the nation, the people – write in a world of justice, mercy, and peace for all humankind.

introduction

On a bus from Jerusalem to Tel Aviv years ago, I gazed at the amazingly green landscape on either side, alive thanks to the same Zionist intention that laid the pavement upon which we were driving. Burnt tanks preserved on the highway shoulder bore testimony to the battles the Jewish People has been forced to and continue to fight to preserve our right to live as a free people in our native land, now known as the State of Israel.

The beauty of the natural landscape and the brutal reminders of the very real cost of freedom have been in my eyes.

Something changed on October 7, 2023. *I think.*

At a recent Shabbat dinner, I remarked on this to a longtime friend who responded with compassion:

> *"Menachem, nothing has changed. This is how it's always been."*

And I wonder. That bus ride and its multivalenced view, perhaps different from the scars in Israel's southern communities only in how recently the wounds were suffered, suggests that my friend was right. The battles of 1948, 1967, and 1973 were but three of countless international attacks on Israel and those who call it home. Both intifadas (1987-1993 and 2000-2005) were constant murderous assaults on Israeli civilians.

Was October 7 anything new? Comparisons to the Shoah have become common, and they are not without merit. Holocaust Survivors danced and cried and sang and marched with Nova Survivors at Auschwitz this past *Yom YaShoah veHaGevurah*. Time has always been fluid in Jewish experience. As Elie Wiesel put it:

> "A Jew lives in more than one place, in more than one era, on more than one level. To be Jewish is to be possessed of a historical consciousness that transcends individual consciousness."[1]

It is too soon to look back at what happened. *It is still happening.*

Perhaps, given the continuity of scars on our soul and our soil and the way Jewish time-consciousness connects all moments, it will never not be present. Our hearts and this place, this beautiful, sacred, holy, complicated place we call home is pervaded by this kind of demanding intensity.

---

[1] *Against Despair*, 1979

I remember sitting on that Hebrew bus on a Hebrew highway with a Hebrew ticket stub in my pocket and Hebrew thoughts in my Hebrew heart. I wouldn't have it any other way.

Israel is where I count myself, bitten and blessed, burnt and inspired, crackling, fierce, and alive.

May these words I could not hold back be worthy.

May our family be whole again, soon and in our days.

Am Yisrael Chai – the People Israel is Alive!

        Menachem Creditor

        8 Iyar 5784
        May 16, 2024

Book One: Before

jerusalem syndrome (in tel aviv)

i sit at history's intersection
gazing at my jewish coffee and croissant,
my meal and i
baked, brewed, served, packaged
by distant sisters and brothers
born of a shared origin
destined to share a collective fate.

i am known fully
only right here,
a corner where the world, for once,
only exists in hebrew translation.

the streets of tel aviv

the streets of tel aviv are so incredibly real.
jewish poets' names on street signs,
playgrounds named for righteous gentiles,
memorials for a slain leader flanked by a
utility cover emblazoned with the name of a
hebrew municipality...

...a mechitza minyan housed in a local secular
high school named for a russian yiddish writer
(who was killed in the warsaw ghetto holding
a copy of the zohar), prayers led by women
and gay men, a room filled with brides and
grooms and babies and scholars and melodies
from a start-up minyan in new york...

as opposed to jerusalem, whose very air is
pervaded by mythic power, the amazing
world of tel aviv is real and gritty, grounded
and reflective of living judaism defined by
living jews making day-to-day life.

i'm not sure which is holier anymore.

crosswalk minyan

perched on this porch
God's name
spelled in leather letters
on my arm and head
i pray with the minyan below
filling streets and crosswalks
driving buses, walking dogs.

to the prayers
their lives comprise
i say amen.

Gnarled Roots in Tel Aviv

From a distance it's all a mess,
haphazard, chaotic, wild,
root upon root
not enough earth
not enough water
boxed in from every side
frozen, dead.

But pavement is itself suspended
far above the living earth
and these thick, gnarled roots
know their ways home.

here alone

i swallow the city whole,
swallowed by the music of its holy stores,
the all of its life.

here, my heart beats.
here, there is no threat
(even when there is).

here i know who i am,
who i was born to be,
to whom i was born.

here.
here alone.

here i know there is stuff,
but that's only the surface,
what can be seen.

holy pizza, holy trinkets,
holy black, brown, and white.
hebrew buses, headscarfs and chumus.
graffiti makes me weep,
even litter warms me.

my childhood stomping ground,
my adult mikveh.

this is my imperfect mirror,
my hard place,
my pulse.

- 3 teens in uniform walk by, then 5 more,
and suddenly i can't breathe -

already i am reflecting from the outside, but
for a moment there, an exquisitely painful
glorious liminal moment, i and my home were
one.

i don't want to leave.
part of me never does.

why do i tremble?

sitting here,
cup of coffee in trembling hand,
i reflect: why do i tremble?
i'm not under threat, am i?

am i?

my brother, my sister,
my mother, my daughter, my son..
they'll be fine, won't they?

how i speak today
is only words,
isn't it?

an interview doesn't save anyone, couldn't
change anything..
could it?

we'll be safe.
we'll be fine.
won't we?

oh...
that's why.

a moment of radical normalcy

i stood on my porch,
set to embark on
pilgrimage to israel,
when a family
from my neighborhood walked by.

their hijabs made me pause.

what if they and i
could be loving neighbors
not only here,
but in our lands of promise?

as i wondered,
one of them called out,
"shalom, "
to which i replied:
"a salaam aleikum."

the children
who are my neighbors
peeked over my fence,
asking their mothers,
"who wished us peace?"

my heart broke with
one simple truth:
i do.

hoping between sobs

crying singing.
hands on the eastern wall of my shul,
touching every shul,
images of bloody tallitot haunt me
as i teach hatikvah to
a new generation of
irrational hopeful jews
(just don't let them see me cry)

begging the cosmos for peace,
knowing it's irrational
demanding it anyway
(between sobs, of course)

two minutes

standing silent
bodies swaying
next to frozen cars
as a national shofar blares

stopping time
transforming
highway into shul
childhood into something else
adults into children
strangers into barrack-mates
citizens into a people
people into survivors
survivors into symbols

swaying insecure
determined to remember
fight and protect
preparing to mourn
struggling for air

never again
will highway be highway
child be child
memory be memory
strangers be strangers

never again
for two minutes

this bench

a soldier who looked like me
walks by the bench
where i sit drinking my morning coffee.

the bench is surrounded
by jewish dumpsters
and jewish buses,
jewish flowers.

the bench has a small sign
affixed to it. the sign reads:

'in memory of our dear mother
hannah hutrer, 1909 - 2004
survivor of the shoah.'

i sit on a survivor's bench
surrounded by jewish flowers.

one year later
or
**looking forward to having less to write
(2015)**

i sit in jerusalem,
one year later.
one year after
bombs, sirens, shelters
the sky feels free of weaponry
faces seem clear of stress.

yes, sky and faces know better,
but, in this moment,
even the sun feels happier.

**committed to home: 5 years, 2 years, and 1 year ago today - and today
(2016)**

I. Five Years Ago

entered yad vashem's valley of the
communities,
saw my ancestral community (moldova) listed,
lost in where/when

staring at a boxcar with suddenly,
intentionally stopped tracks
that today point to
(and, oy, would that they had led to)
the forests of jerusalem.
no words...
my heart is devastated once again.

a grandson, dear soul, spoke of his
grandparents' legacy as partizans from
vilna. when we recited the el maleh (prayer
for memory), we added the words "those
who fought" to the passive "those who were
murdered."

moved, afraid, pulled by
the commitment to act

the irony (and tactile education) at yad vashem of being forced to wait in lines to watch footage of jews waiting in line...

I pass guided tours in hebrew, english, german, spanish by teen-aged guides to thousands of visitors. how can memory be translated? shared? preserved?

watching ethopian israeli soldiers training visiting the fallen at har herzl cemetery

leadership, sacrifice, and the unity of the Jewish People in the face of national trauma? what would herzl say of israel today? what internal/external nation-building remains?

returning from extraordinary home hospitality in tekoa. troubled beyond words, trying to reconcile human warmth and the unfathomable readiness to dehumanize another type of person, based on years of violence and trauma.

but isn't that the case on every side?

II. Two Years Ago

Felt the heartbeat of the stones.
Delivered notes from my students.
Promised I'd be back soon.
Rockets overhead.

A Prayer for Right Now:

> *Dear God, Source of Life,*
> *May every human being on earth*
> *live without fear.*
> *May my family be safe tonight.*
> *May both prayers, O God,*
> *be fulfilled in the same moment,*
> *a moment that lasts for all eternity.*
>
> *Dear One, I am clinging to hope,*
> *crying, trying not to lose my grip*
> *from the wetness of all our tears.*
>
> *May we see glimmers of hope*
> *here, there, and beyond any borders,*
> *soon and in our days.*
> *Amen.*

I pray to the Oneness that Binds Creation to itself, and name that Oneness "God." There are infinite names for that Force that leads the world through Love.

Sharing the Name for that Oneness is a delight, and no claim borne of Love lessens my experience of the One whose Name is Love.

III. One Year Ago

Women of the Wall: Haredim yelling curses at the start of the month when we mourn the destruction of the Temple, caused by hatred. Irony? We don't need internal enemies, we'll just self-destruct as a People.

Too many experiences to name in scant pre-Shabbes moments. Dizzying demanding demonstrations of the dignity of difference. #MyZionism

IV: Today

Flying home from home,
feeling the weight of history,
the despair of history,
the power of history.

Reeling from testimony from inspiring Jewish and Arab thought leaders, exhausted by non-stop learning, grateful for a stunning Shabbat in Jerusalem. Hearing the wisdom of rabbis and Israeli LGBTQ leaders, Palestinian visionary builders, respectful Knesset opponents, civil rights activists...

Just heard that hours after I took leave from my colleagues, a terrorist was stopped in Jerusalem before being able to murder with a bomb. On the same block they shared a falafel and delightful Saturday night together.

I promised the Western Wall stone I've now
visited 28 times, a stone whose devotees
don't call me rabbi, that I'm coming home
again soon.

Heart in the East,
body heading West,
committed to hope,
committed to Home.

68 Words, 68 Years
(2016)

From the fiery furnace we rose
knowing what it is to be hated,
Jewish blood spilled
every century
every continent
hasn't erased our hope,
to be free, to be a blessing.

Wielding weapons we wish we didn't need,
we fight with tears in our eyes,
praying that same prayer we've always
prayed:
peace.

What new songs will we teach our precious
children?

Our home, our land, our choice.

still there
in memory of ezra schwartz z"l

this past week
as full,
as hard,
as rich,
as trying as any we've known.

and: stars shine in tonight's sky.
far too many precious souls
have joined the array.
their reflected light,
brighter than ever,
glistens on our wet cheeks.

and: eyes meet,
shared tears reminding us all
of our hearts,
that they're still there,
still beating,
still feeling,
still grieving,
still hoping.

and: so much more to do
before we can rest.
we can do it.
we must.

we will hope
that better day into reality,
crying together.

defiant rugelach

i hadn't come back,
more than a decade since
the bomb.

burned by hate,
baptized by blood and tears,
rebuilt in weeks,
memorial plaque installed in months,
sbarros became ma'afeh ne'eman,
(bakery of faith)
where life and rugelach
are delicious, dammit,
and refuse to stop.

echoes of that horrid blast
fill my earseyesheartsoul
as i sit here once again
and defiantly enjoy my pastry.

ice cream prophets
(2013)
in support of jewish students at uc berkeley

misguided good-intention
threatens my family tonight.

i am a jew,
standing in the same spot
i stood three years ago.
new faces scream
the same old claims of being silenced
and through their screaming seek to silence.

these anti-israel students with ice cream sundaes
claim prophecy
and the right to speak for the oppressed.
surreal. cartoon. a rerun, even.
delusion with serious consequence.

campus is a high school rally tonight,
applause indicating
popularity/righteousness/rightness.
fashionable activism in place of mindful engagement
for the sake of peace.

clap, clap.

silence?
good conversation - real conversation,
happening everywhere but here tonight.
one side claims exclusive rights to empathy
and the other points to facts and complexity.
no one's listening, just taking turns.
this doesn't resemble community in the
slightest.

a fourth-year points to her ethnic ancestry
and claims "i know what it's like to be
oppressed."
who doesn't? and who on campus could?
oppressed as she high-fives a sorority sister?
and who, through ancestors, doesn't embody
a painful past?

too many tears this week for everyone
everywhere.
why create more?

A Prayer After a Terror Attack in a Jerusalem Synagogue on International Holocaust Remembrance Day (January 27, 2023)

Today, on a day when the world too late
acknowledges the 6 million,
offers eloquent words about saving Jews,
who will cry out for the blood of 7 of us,
shot in a Jerusalem synagogue while praying?

Or will headlines mitigate murder
by pointing to politics
or which area of Jerusalem the shul was in?

Is Jewish blood only tragic
when it's in the right neighborhood
or decades ago?

Today is the day the world remembers the Holocaust
because it is the day they showed up,
years into known Genocide.

Today, as Jews are slaughtered in shul
and headlines minimize the horror,
we are reminded that
no one showed up for years
while Jewish blood ran like a river through
pristine shopping districts
and Jewish ashes fell on neat European homesteads.

Jews remember the Holocaust
on the day we fought back.
Jews remember every day.
Because today's terrorist
first shot an elderly woman in the street.
Then shot a motorcycle rider.
Then entered the sanctuary and fired at
worshippers.
All Jews.
Wherever we are.

Today the world is witness
to its ongoing Jewish problem.
But today, grieving,
we do not wait for their solution.
Today's horror isn't truly news.
Today's horror is why
the Jewish homeland matters.

Because, as we chant in the Torah this week:
Where we go, we go with
"with our young and our old" (Ex. 10:9).
None of us expendable.
We are a global family
who knows today's news all too well,
deep in our bones.

We will Never Forget.
Not our 7 fallen sisters and brothers.
Not our 6 million lost sisters and brothers.
We will never forget
what we must remember.

tears and hope
with deep gratitude
to Jewish educators everywhere

their faces, shining, beautiful, scared,
looking to me for reassurance
when i have
none to offer.

so i hold back my tears
and share my hopes for peace
and a memory of being
right where they were
when i was their age,

afraid for family & friends,
hoping for their safety,
wondering what i'm doing
so far from home.

and once the children leave
my defenses crumble
because

i never stopped being their age.
and my family hasn't yet know peace.

and calling out to God
only makes me
cry more.

j. l. gordon st: a one-street poem

i wander.
just a normal morning walk
past coffee shops and cracked pavement,
pedestrians, dogs, and bicycles.

i lift up my eyes.
"miklat tzibori/public bomb shelter"
on a sign over an agency
for handicapped children.

i wonder:
can any morning walk
under such a reminder
be normal?

i lift up my eyes.
a construction site
for an already-sold out
apartment building,
a crane overhead
bearing its burden.

i wonder:
has ever before
been dreamt into reality
such a holy tool,
capable of defying
the very ground upon which it stands?

i lift up my eyes.
the ocean,
crashing as it always has,
salt and water, remnants of
all that has ever been
all that is
all that will ever be.

i wander
down still-soft pavement,
remove my shoes,
revel in soft, warm sand,
soak in glorious sunshine,
rejoice at the sounds,
of my children's laughter.

and i know:
we are the cracked pavement,
the salt and the water,
the shelter and the laughter...

wandering.
wondering.
eyes. always. lifted. up.

Jerusalem at 6am (2016)

I. The Cyclist of King David St.

Thinning, cropped hair,
dark skin over Eastern European features,
he passes me by,
rolling downhill,
inscrutable expression on his face.

Is it my tallis and tefillin bag? My American
sandals? Perhaps it's that he noticed me
noticing him.

Maybe he's just a man enjoying his morning
ride, and being in Israel fills my eyes with
Jewish meaning.

II. Davening in a Secret Garden

Purple.
Fuchsia?
Definitely not pink.
Glowing, growing all around.

Strings from my tallis
dangle and sway,
suspended over newly-placed
Jerusalem stone.

I choose to daven
just yards from the Old City.
It's more colorful here.

III. Almost Home

Almost there, I tell myself.
Just over that next hill,
and I'll be home,
safe and sound.

Walking is good, I tell myself.
Wandering is exploring,
the chance to take in new surroundings,
learn, adapt, and respond.

I'm so busy convincing myself the road ahead
is clear and safe, I trip over a rusty metal
plate in the sidewalk, reminding me where to
place any bomb I might see.

aromatics: the jerusalem syndrome

part i: "just to say my name"

i sit at the cafe,
overwhelmed just listening
to the names being called
to pick up each order.
how many times have i had to spell my name
(or invent a more anglo-sounding one)
when ordering something?

and here i sit,
unable to even begin a delicious coffee
through my tears
for having my name recognized, accepted,
pronounced correctly?

suddenly,
at cafe aroma at the malcha mall
in jerusalem,
crying into my coffee,
i remember i'm home.

part ii: "my prophetess has a tattoo"

my prophetess has a tattoo.
she doesn't even know
that she's awoken my soul.

so casually she repeated my name,
and went to get me a croissant,
then turned away.

later i glanced at her,
noticing the tattoo on her shoulder,
and i smiled.

the prophetess of aroma
brought me what i needed,
without knowing herself
through my eyes.

part iii: "a new kotel"

they say the western wall still stands
because all of israel built it -
children, men, women.

it isn't the priests' wall, nor the artisan's wall.
it is the people's construction,
the construction of the people.

i look up and see the dishwasher,
the barista, the soldier, the businessman,
all on their cell phones,
building themselves and those
on the other end of the line.

is that "only" people's expressions,
of the expression of a people,
brick by brick?

part iv: "eretz tropit (remix)"

the first time it played,
i looked up and smiled,
a decade's memories flooding back.

i sang that song, i thought,
and it brought me back
to intoxicating days of music.

and so i began to write.

thirty minutes later
it played again.

are my precious memories
a jewish kind of holiday mix?

part v: "reflection"

something makes me look up.
i see the mirror,
and my own intense glance,
captured, framed, and returned.

am i a part of this scene?

might another be describing
a barista, a soldier,
and a contemplative rabbi,
furiously scribbling in the back of his book?

is this normalized jewish bustle
in need of the meaning i see and seek?
or is this bustle normalized jewish meaning
itself?

Our Cherished Litany of Loss
(2017)

You, Jerusalem,
(God, Your name burns my mouth.)
golden watch-towers,
heart-pulsing sacred stones,
center of the universe,
lion's share of all the beauty that could be...

millions clamor for Your love...
...You, O Jerusalem

Eternal City, why do You sit alone?

I miss You so very much.
I miss You in Your absence,
long for You because You are not here,
because I am not there, with You.
That is about me,
not about you.
I mourn for myself when I mourn for You.

Just now,
I walked Your streets,
wept at your renewed splendor and excessive spenders,
cried over the ruins and the ruined people
who adorn You.

Stones without end absorb us all,
joyful shouts and fallen souls,

estranged brothers and sisters,
inches away from each other's hearts.

Hidden are the Divine ledgers of sin,
but lists upon lists of right and wrong
are still kept
(those ancient stones have witnessed it all):

smothered sigh and fierce anger,
ignited faith and craven hunger,
brokenness artistry ecstasy and light

build burn burned dance
eat eaten ...eaten

Jerusalem Jerusalem
You poor, aching city,
You spread Your worn hands for help,
but there are no comforters
who truly listen.

You sitting alone under all of us
is all of us sitting alone
under and on-top of each other.

Two Temples,
Nine days,
three weeks,
sixty-seven
two-thousand,
six million,
all numbers,
our cherished litany of loss.

You call to all Your lovers,
but we, one of your beloved lovers,
hear only our own name.

But today's strange gift
longing for what is already restored...

Might we finally remember
to cease pretending we own
Your Infinite beauty,
that Your ruin is our own making?
Haven't we mourned enough to learn
that we belong to You,
not the other way 'round?

Turn us that we might return,
for we have forgotten
Jerusalem
(You burn me)

mall poems

i. looking up

battery dead, i look up:
children in bumper cars,
just another day at the mall.
parents jostling to get their child
this pink car, that blue one.

one boy with a kippah (in the pink car)
crashes into a girl's (purple) car
and smiles.

their parents don't stand together.
one's mom here, the other's there.
she wears a sheitel. she wears a hijab.

when the children collide and smile
i search their mothers' eyes,
but they're looking down,
distracted by their phones.

ii. sof onah / end of the season

discounts glare from every angle,
people everywhere, noise everywhere.

an arab family walks into hoodies,
followed by two yeshiva bochers.
a father carries his young girl,
a mother searches the crowd for hers.

i sit under an hd samsung tv, watching it all,
pushed by the noise, lights, chaos, lostness,
and the rush of undifferentiated humanity, all
just trying to to find a sale, their sale.

iii. a bag for eggs

twenty-three years ago
my father gave me a mesh bag for eggs,
for when i would go shopping.

the bag was already yellowed with age,
the bagless world it served long gone.

here, in this jewish mall,
cellphone kiosks abound,
flanked by american eagle and children's place,
cafe hillel and nautica,
pizza hut and toys r us.

i just ordered an omelette,
bought an extra cellphone battery,
and a new pair of sandals.

i brought my own bag.

iv. tzomet hasefarim / book junction

an image comes to mind
here in this brought, hebrew bookstore:
five weathered books, stacked carefully

on my office bookshelf,
a gift from my father,
torah with rashi.

as i plow through an aharon appelfeld novel,
surrounded by all these shiny new books,
those faded blue volumes
fill my eyes.

v. the mall

i didn't come here
searching for meaning.
it's a mall, after all.

but.

the escalator and elevator
carry God's images up and down.
a child sits by a gushing fountain
built of rock, with his mother.
spices and silver (and much more) are traded here.

voices echo and combine,
bouncing off each surface,
rising to the domed sapphire roof,
perhaps beyond.

i... i did not know.

the prophets' boutique
(2017)

walk with me
through downtown Jerusalem
this Friday afternoon
see through these wide, crying eyes
the miraculous art
of Ben Gurion's dreams:

Hebrew lotto signs
ever-present Jewish cranes
King George's great synagogue
(though the truly great ones
never need to say so)

can't take one step
not even one
without noticing it all

manhole covers and exquisite flowers
spikey signs and rabbinic schwarma
overwhelm me

years ago, I sat right here
soldiers and Pre-Shabbat shoppers
passing by (maybe the same ones!)

I wept then and weep now
over their very existence
each of them a treasure.

(three Israeli girls just asked two chabadniks if
they could put on tefilin. that's new.)

King David could have never imagined
the prophets' boutique
he founded.

I just can't stop seeing
can barely imagine blinking
I'd miss something

These broken stones feel somehow stable
beneath my feet. They're always shifting,
always slightly unstable, but today, right now,
holy ground holds and grounds me.

It's just so good to be home.

missing my own heartbeat

aching, weeping
thousands of miles
from my own soul

wondering
why i am
so far from home

limbs abound
but my jewish body is stronger
when it can hear its own heartbeat

Kotel Poem

answers, nonstop answers
batter ancient stones
eroded by unceasing assent:
amen! amen! amen! amen!
I sit, facing my old friend,
broken stone who's absorbed
my tears, prayers, anger, sadness, ecstasy
this warm-hearted friend
who's felt my children's caresses.
I sit for a while, to find my questions.
It starts to rain, as if to say:
go home - that's where
you'll find your answers.

Book Two: October 7

A Prayer from a Traumatized Jewish Heart
Rabbi Menachem Creditor

Oh, God
Our eyes, our eyes
Our hearts, our hearts
Our children, our children
Our mothers, our mothers
Our elders, our parents
Our teachers, our grandchildren
Our warriors, our peacekeepers
Our very souls…

….it is more than we can bear,
and it only gets worse
with every photo and every video.

God, protect our children from the images emblazoned now in our eyes and minds, from the worst nightmare to ever befall the Jewish People. Our enemy, the face of real evil, seeks to destroy our family, body and soul.

We must be like steel. We must be like iron. But we must never lose our warm and loving hearts along the way. We will fight until they are all erased from under the face of the Heavens. We have no choice. They have shown us what they will do if we do not. They've already perpetrated unfathomable evil. And we will force the world to bear witness as we reel with pain.

God, protect our protectors,
who are only children,
our children fighting for our future.
Shield them as they serve
as the sword we hate to need.
Hold our hearts.
Let us not become hard like stone
as we do what we must to save our lives.

Amen.

What I See
10.15.23

I see
my own face,
the faces of my ancestors
in black and white,
hands up, behind barbed wire,
in pits.

I see
the candle lit
at the door of the oven
in Poland
i placed it there when I was 17

I see
1,300 candles lit
at the fountain
in Tel Aviv
my sister's family lives there now

I see
weddings and funerals
body bags and body bags and
body bags and weddings
and babies and survivors
and blood, oh so much blood
I see blood

I see
there really is evil in the world
and there are people calling it just
(were there rallies in 1942 for the Nazis
on college campuses?)

I see
words and words
and words and words
and flags and blood
and graves and babies...

I see
that I cannot see
the world I thought I saw

I see
that we must fight
for our babies

I see
what our ancestors saw

I see
we are all survivors now

I am a survivor
I see

Fractals of the Broken
1.17.24

too many tears
each one a fractal
of the broken:

136 missing + 103 days
hundreds violated
thousands murdered
millions accused.

add them all
and then
multiply them
to the Infinite Power

**Upon Bearing Testimony to Atrocities
Committed Against Am Yisrael**
1.19.24

Healer of Shattered Souls,
we ask that You notice us
and all those who have promised
to bear testimony
to unspeakable horrors.

The indelible marks with which
these images and sounds
will scar us to our cores
are permanent.
We will never
unsee nor unhear
any of this.
We accept this terrible imperative.

We bear witness
to honor the dead

Women
Men
Boys
Girls
Grandmothers
Grandfathers
Whole families
Babies

whose bodies were violated
whose very humanity was denied.

We affirm,
through this sacred witnessing,
that they were in fact
human beings,
created in Your Image,
worthy of infinite dignity.

God,
Who has Witnessed
all of this for all time,
we beg You send Divine Warmth
to reanimate us
when our eyes
are full of this darkness,
to somehow reinflate our souls
when breathing feels wrong.

Remind us to fight for joy,
for that is what the souls
we witness today deserved,
what every human being deserves.

May the memories of our martyrs be forever blessed.
May Am Yisrael, the Jewish People, heal and rebuild and find heart once again.

Upon My Heart
11.20.23

my heart keeps breaking
so I grip it and feel something hard
pressed up against it.
and I know. I've always known
but I know differently now.
I hear my family's heartbeat
when I sleep and when I wake,
walking on the way and sitting at home.

Listen, Israel:
I place these words
between my eyes
and upon my heart.

#bringthemhomenow

Nova Poem #1
1.23.24

Yes, we will dance again -
once we remember
how to breathe.

but for now,
we fight for the right
to be seen as human,
worthy of the right to breathe.
then, we'll dance.

(maybe we won't wait.)

The State of our Heart
2.11.24

hundreds of days later
always on the verge of tears
we refuse to forget
we refuse to let anyone
in this mad world forget

so here we are
screaming across kilometers
into the darkness below
to our grandfathers and grandmothers
to our daughters and sons
to feel our desperate love
to hold onto life in the face of terror
to know that we are fighting them
and that, out of our love for them all,
we will not stop

this is the state of our heart

this is not the end
2.14.2024

Oh, crucible -
terrifying tunnels,
weaponized identity
of lostness and rage

frightening reminders
that, despite having returned home
ending 2,00 years of exile,
things have not truly changed.
not for for the Jew.
not yet.

but we have not fallen.
we are hurt,
wounded to our core.
but
this is not the end.

it was our burning history of falling
that raised us up into
warriors who could raise ourselves up

no longer looking to heaven for salvation
or, perhaps, simply not waiting for God to send a savior,
we transformed into saviors ourselves,
so that, when the next enemy arose,
our children would not see our shoulders slump.

our children now witness something changed.
something we changed about ourselves.

yes, despite this crucible,
we have not fallen.
we faced history's fires
and, defiant,
decided to stop waiting
for the world to change.

it did not.
so we did.

for our children's children,
we are not fallen.
we do not fall.

Am.
Yisrael.
Chai.

So That They Will See
3.13.24

In the middle of Grand Central
I adjust my scarf
so that they will see
our son,
whom I carry

Nova Poem #2
5.7.24

Nova 06:29.
Today.
Seven months.

these images are so hard.
i will never unsee them.
the footage is so intense.
i am witness.
the sounds are etched in my ears.
i will not ignore what I heard.

so beautiful, this tribe of love.
they were so beautiful.
shimmering as they danced,
each and every one.

we're going to have to be
beautiful for them.
we're going to have to
love in their names.

October Rain ("Hurricane")
05.12.2024

today's tears course through ragged rivulets,
long-dried tracks of ancestors in a desert
yet other ancestors caused to bloom.
an eternal river runs deep
beneath the heart of it
nourishing the seeds of every generation's
garden of Eden.

Rabbi Menachem Creditor serves as the Pearl and Ira Meyer Scholar in Residence at UJA-Federation New York and was the founder of Rabbis Against Gun Violence. An acclaimed author, scholar, and speaker with over 4 million views of his online videos and essays, he was named by Newsweek as one of the fifty most influential rabbis in America. His numerous books and 6 albums of original music include the global anthem *Olam Chesed Yibaneh* and the COVID-era 2-volume anthology *When We Turned Within*. He and his wife Neshama Carlebach live in New York, where they are raising their five children. Find out more at menachemcreditor.net.

Alden Solovy is a modern day *piytan*, a traveling poet/preacher/teacher who uses Torah and verse to engage and inspire. Alden embodies the intersection of scholarship and heart. His writings resonate with soul and his presence is sought after in Jewish spiritual spaces around the world. Alden's work challenges the boundaries between poetry, song, meditation, personal growth, storytelling, and prayer. His teaching spans from Jerusalem to Vancouver, including HUC-JIR, the Conservative Yeshiva, Leo Baeck College, and synagogues throughout North America. His fifth volume from CCAR Press – *Enter These Gates: Meditations for the Days of Awe* – is forthcoming in 2024. His other CCAR Press books are: *These Words: Poetic Midrash on the Language of Torah* (2023), *This Grateful Heart: Psalms and Prayers for a New Day* (2017), *This Joyous Soul: A New Voice for Ancient Yearnings* (2019), and *This Precious Life: Encountering the Divine with Poetry and Prayer* (2021). *These Words* won a Silver Medal from the Independent Book Publishers. His work appears in more than 25 collections, including CCAR Press books: *Mishkan Ga'avah: Where Pride Dwells* (2020); *The Year of Mourning: A Jewish Journey* (2023); and *Prophetic Voices: Renewing and Reimagining Haftarah* (2023). Alden made Aliyah to Jerusalem in 2012, where he is Liturgist in Residence at the Pardes Institute of Jewish Studies. Find his latest works at www.tobendlight.com.